ACCOLADES

Donald A. Schaberg

It Is "ACCOLADE TIME"

Within our period of space and time, summaries of events, circumstances, and personal observations and inspirations have come to me in poetic form. Rather than let them pass and be forgotten, I thought a few should be recorded as the world spins into the next century. Each lyric or poem contains and relates to an upbeat message of recognition and tribute with something of a periscopic view, seeking out the best and the most positive aspect of each subject reviewed.

ISBN: 0-9651390-1-8
Library of Congress Catalog Number: 96-92013
Copyright (1996 by Donald Arthur Schaberg

Published by: Donald Arthur Schaberg
                  1830 North Grand River
                  Lansing, Michigan 48906-3905
                  Fax and Phone: 517-487-9100
                  Printed in the United States of America

As an artist paints a subject, building, or setting, this accolader (poet) has written a playful format of words to help you appreciate and enjoy the energies that occur in the space around us. A gentleman professor has noted that the writer enjoys creating these insights and words and even ones that jump through hoooooops . . . "Oooooops," he says, "now you have me doing it!" So be it. . . .

CONTENTS

ACCOLADES

His assignment was not a difficult one—read and prepare a video presentation on one of the great poets of the twentieth century. The lad scrolls through the library's computerized index screen, passing all the familiar names that his classmates would surely have taken. Procrastination always has its price!

Accolades. What in the world? He removes a credit-card-size dictionary from his shirt pocket and scans it over the little book's title. An instant later the card speaks: "Accolade: Recorded tribute and description of a person, event, or acknowledgment."

The lad locates the worn book on a lower shelf in the back of the library. He hadn't noticed the author's name on the index screen, but now, holding the book in his hands, it jumps out at him. It's his great, great, great, great grandfather!

The memories, as captured on disk and handed down over the years, come back in a flood. Don Schaberg, with his wife, Mary Lou, and their six children, twenty grandchildren, and many more to follow, contributed greatly to their communities. His work as a lumber executive, his hobbies and interests—architecture, photography, travel, participation in sports—all left lasting impressions of the people and places he encountered.

The young lad opens the book and immediately finds himself engrossed. Settling into a comfortable chair, he delights in the author's observations of a time long past.

I hope you will, too.

Jack

COMMUNITY

LITTLE GUY

Let's give some praise to the little guy with drive—
The one who has worked so hard to survive.

Born and raised under all conditions,
Educated by schooling, experience, and many traditions.

Hard working, honest, dedicated, and expecting the best,
Facing the ever-changing world along with the rest.

Trying to figure out the next step to take,
Meeting with others, trying not to make a mistake.

With support from his wife, children, and others,
Many hope for growth in working with their brothers.

Testing emotions, attitudes, and wills along the way,
They often want to break even and live another day.

Most who work have grown beyond past generations,
Enjoying material benefits and caring relations.

Their situations, causes, directions, and time
Sometimes have to be helped by others in the climb.

As unseen and uncertain economic changes take place,
They need to adjust and adapt to save face.

And yet how blessed, overall, through planning they are,
Always thinking, working, and hoping to find a lucky star.

January 1995

AMERICA'S AUTOMOBILE

Be thankful, be thankful, friends who are on the move,
While that convenient vehicle waits for you to approve.

For a moment, let us think about that marvelous
automobile,
Which transports our bodies with unbounded zeal.

It is that enclosed machine we drive with pride—
With its power, great handling, and comfortable ride.

Be grateful, be grateful, for heaven's gift on wheels
As it whisks us about and keeps us on even keels.

Remember the toil and the latest engineering advances for
traveling ease,
Maneuvering us, yet flexible enough to squeeze past the
breeze.

Carrying out millions of hurried missions each and every
day,
And providing the working contributors with their needed
pay.

Super mobile cars with many buttons, levers, handles,
and lights,
Beautiful music and communications—somewhat like
roadway satellites.

These colorful, sculptured, flowing cars are doing their
      part;
How can we ever thank the manufacturers who built them
      to start?

And thanks from all the licensed drivers who respect the
      highway truce—
Congratulations for 100 years of producing automobiles for
      our happy use.

January 1, 1996

THE EMPLOYERS

Honors to employers—the ones who lead and guide;
They set the team on the right course and seldom chide.

Sometimes they are gifted with the time and role,
Destined to work and set a high goal.

Constantly investing and holding on to succeed,
The objective is to create, find a market, and satisfy a need.

Dealing with the concerns that come day by day,
Asking for faith to direct the way.

Aware of understanding and the role of responsibility,
They are endowed with superior utility.

Challenged to risk their product, status, reputation, and
    service,
Striving to benefit others without becoming too nervous.

Meeting the payroll and staying on track,
Maintaining their reputation by handling the flack.

Brilliance, courage, drive, hard work, and desire
Appear to be the talents that light their fire.

Along with the team, good people, and persistence applied,
We should remember the employers and how hard they
    tried.

THOSE WHO SERVE

The purpose is to have the will of the people satisfied,
To maintain a fine community and have its consensus
    ratified.

The requirement of government is to create balance and
    direction;
Functioning systems vote for that hope in each election.

We need a chief executive to manage the township structure
So that social issues and business interests do not rupture.

Sunday schools end their problems with solutions,
Beginning with love and understanding as their
    resolutions.

The community is larger than each of us,
So leaders must search beyond ego for people's trust.

Open minds, reason, and determination are what it takes—
Debates, decisions, and then friendly handshakes.

These are just a few observations for consideration;
Come on now, everyone, let's think of the next generation.

You are soon a part of history as you release judgment's file;
You can resolve problems with confidence and a warm smile.

We have had a good government and a system that is
    working;
Please let us continue to keep our community perking.

September 6, 1994

LEGOS LEAD THE WAY

What an enduring legacy Legos are for our time,
Allowing the child's imagination to climb.

Magnificently creative, constructive, and colorful,
Keeping thousands of minds and fingers powerful.

The plastic block Legos have charmed many nations,
Giving countless families many home vacations.

Years ago in Athens, Greece, a studded system was used
When Godfred Christiansen built a connection like Zeus.

Each Lego becomes a fabulous, educational building block.
Next may come a fantasy palace for the imperial gardens in
    Bangkok.

The sounds of these pieces, when they are scattered about,
Have been known to make some parents shout.

As the Lego team works to achieve quality with inspiration,
Thanks for a great Danish contribution for many a
    generation.

<u>ROTARY</u>

Rotary is one of the greatest clubs in the world.
Members take time from their daily routines to be unfurled.

What qualities make Rotarians so unique?
First, into their principles we must take a peek.

Truthfulness, fairness, good will, and friendships are all
    beneficial;
This is the Rotary creed—it is official.

Service and fellowship are the constant goal.
Oh, if all people could aspire to a similar role.

The Rotary purpose is one of many great causes.
Where would people be without these patient pauses?

And so may all of life's cycles revolve like the Rotary wheel,
To give our life's journey a better feel.

April 11, 1986

ACCOLADES FOR THE CLERGY

There are many dedicated people in the clergy,
It's a blessing they did not go into metallurgy.

These are the compassionate leaders of our inward peace,
Uniting the world's inhabitants in a holy masterpiece.

Caring, listening, and guiding our inward beings
Into the realm of righteous feelings.

Churches, synagogues, and temples are the places of
     teaching,
Where the sacred books are within each one's reaching.

Praying that we may all have a better understanding
To create a virtuous life for a smoother landing.

The clergy counsel, console, and uplift human souls,
Applying the scriptures in numerous roles.

So as these religious leaders enlighten our way,
May our hearts be grateful for how they selflessly pray.

May 31, 1995

HEROES

On New Year's Eve in December 1994,
We reminisced about the 1940s war.

So many of our young men were involved there;
They served in many ways, surrounded by risk and dare.

The personnel, campaigns, and trials of concern
Became one of history's major periods to yearn

For peace, freedom, victory, and order.
Our nation's mission was also to have a calm, secure
    border.

The memories of those in the field, air, and sea
Keep returning and are as real as can be.

Oh! So many heroes, yet many stories remain untold,
But that is as it should be when those times grow old.

We again express our gratitude for those who gave their all
So that we, the blessed, can live in freedom's port of call.

New Year's Eve 1994

THANKS TO JOHN CANTLON

Spontaneous and enthusiastic John Cantlon,
The fellow with the nuclear-waste wand.

Indicating current conditions of nuclear waste,
He has aroused our interest with factual taste.

His major concern is disposing of residue fission
For the Nuclear Waste Technical Review Board's mission.

John Cantlon has researched this urgent need;
His leadership is a welcome, momentous deed.

Working with many cultures and various views,
He applies patience while time pays the dues.

There exist many hidden appreciations of thanks
For his willingness and energy in undertaking this task.

All that uranium power with U-235-absorbing neutrons
forming energy
To serve its purpose and then to provide safety for eternity.

Somehow our intuition will ease the way
By guiding decisions for the earth's future in the Milky Way.

We wish to express our continuing gratitude for your
explorations
And your contemporaries' role in planning this for all
nations.

Those happy little atoms never sought all this fuss;
Minute and, when active, they thought life was just a plus.

December 5, 1995

12

EXPERIMENTS IN ACTION

What an appreciative scientific thrill it was to see
The youngsters exhibiting on their way to be.

In their experiments in the fields of chemistry and science,
Many students carefully demonstrated the laws of
compliance.

There was fun and fascination in discovering the hows and
whys,
With balloons and bubbles reacting to a gaseous surprise.

Test tubes of liquids and containers of gas
All performed small miracles with such high class.

The solids became fluids possessing molecular mobility.
What displays of magical nobility!

How many great inventions came from hours of devotion.
Originating in laboratories with patience's potion?

All the mixed colors passed their test
As they worked together and combined for the best.

As pressures of energetic forces astound the scientific
community,
These students learn the right way to bring about unity.

These actions play a part in our timeless universe,
In which the next generation is usefully immersed.

HABITAT FOR HUMANITY

Who are these dedicated people in our pleasant community,
Giving hours of work for their fellow man's unity?

They are the quiet volunteers who recognize a need;
With vision, work, and purpose they will succeed.

Their mission is building houses and improving the
    neighborhood,
Opening hope and opportunity for ownership, which is
    good.

From state to state and in many lands,
Habitat for Humanity is in capable hands.

Cheers to our leading individuals and their directions,
Assembling committed helpers, materials, and collections.

Smiles and happiness from the new owners
Make it worthwhile for the hard-working donors.

Thanks, then, for your great strides and constant vigilance.
Many deserving families are grateful for your diligence.

September 27, 1993

A VALENTINE'S DAY ODE TO ALL
VOLUNTEERS

Sports are for great fun in winning;
Valentine's Day is for gracious giving.

Life's gift to us is a role to lead;
This mission follows for all to succeed.

As worldly causes and concerns have evolved,
Patience and effort rule until they are solved.

And now it is Valentine's Day, when we exchange special
     love,
Sending heartfelt notes, some by fleeting dove.

Happy hearts work on forgiving and understanding;
Some rougher ones could use a little sanding.

The King of Hearts now leaves the deck
To bestow credit due to volunteers by the peck.

Happy Valentine's Day, then, to these caring souls.
We thank them sincerely for their service and unselfish
     goals.

February 14, 1992

ARCHITECTURE

OUR ADVENTURE

In search of the beautiful and the true,
My wife and I found Taliesin in view.

It was there we visited with architect Frank Lloyd Wright,
An individual with creative wisdom and vast insight.

Our need was for a modest family home;
We were young and, at that time, alone.

After months of patiently waiting for our plans,
The original design arrived from Mr. Wright's hands.

The floor-plan sketch in color became our dream;
Brick, glass, steel, and wood combined to form our theme.

Our architect and genius, Frank Lloyd Wright,
Envisioned a perfect living space for our delight.

It is a fortress within nature, and with its flowing freedom
Welcomes all new discoveries as one makes them.

As a complete work of art blended into a perfect home,
It appears at its best from the tower dome.

This is the way it happened—the quest and the reward—
We are most happy and glad we explored!

April 10, 1993

AMERICA'S SECOND PIONEERS

We were the clients who lived in Frank Lloyd Wright's
    world,
Who requested and commissioned, and whose houses
    unfurled.

An architect who explored, dreamed, and designed new
    space,
Discovering unique ideas for each original living place.

Now, this area he uncovered is not close to the stars,
But right here on earth, many miles from distant Mars.

There is no darkness, nor meteorites passing by,
Just remarkable buildings with light far from the sky.

Interiors with a warm, calm, and unified feeling,
Exciting each day with homespun fun, while always
    appealing.

Expressing sensations of grandeur and humbling grace,
Our homes are in nature's garden for use of its inner space.

Frank Lloyd Wright conceived houses that remind one of
    cosmic rooms,
Yet they could be castles, cabins, cathedrals, or heavenly
    blooms.

Giving a spiritual presence in our part of the Milky Way,
Blending into a gravitational power that makes one want to
    stay.

The concrete, brick, steel, stone, and wood
Would proudly attest to this truth if they could.

Then the owners would have proof of a new and
    magnificent space,
Where they, as America's SECOND PIONEERS, have
    shared their home base.

October 14, 1993

OUR HOME

"Oh, what a beautiful home you have—
Beyond description," said the young lad.

Built of brick, steel, concrete, wood, and glass,
Complementing the land with its sculptured mass.

Surrounded by cedars, pines, maples, and oak trees
In Michigan's four seasons with homey ease.

What makes this unique home a living dream?
It is the artistic, spacious rooms with high esteem.

The warm interior with a natural flow
Raises the human spirit with an organic glow.

The grandfather clock chimes the time,
Remembering the architect who designed the Guggenheim.

What a remarkable man, Frank Lloyd Wright,
One who designed an original building for each site.

Creating shelters within landscapes beyond belief,
Challenging them all and even the chief.

Transcending economic cycles and many a temptation,
Then reaching greatness with a renowned reputation.

Thanks to desire, patience, persistence, and time,
As these qualities are applied, they become refined.

July 30, 1989

OH, GOLDEN MORN IN OUR HOME

A golden October morning in Michigan was present;
Its entry was bright and truly resplendent.

As I gazed through our windows at the wonders of fall,
Each tree on the horizon looked like a rainbow-hued ball.

The lush green rolling hills were forever flowing,
While the sunlight and shadows were proudly showing.

A Leica clearness of an exposed setting of splendor,
Surpassed only by a confetti cake mixed in a blender.

The open terrace doors let in the soft, warm wind;
One could hear and see many songbirds in an autumn spin.

At the base of the hill, many sleek deer approach;
Even the young ones could pull Santa's coach.

Another glorious day with flickering and falling leaves,
Certainly another fun attraction, we believe.

The sculptured, tidewater red cypress window frames
Complemented Nature's display before Jack Frost's
    approaching games.

A serene time when you could feel the harmony of autumn,
There were quietly gliding, colorful leaves; we could
    applaud them.

On the table was a large pumpkin waiting for a face;
Our younger daughter would prepare it for its new place.

What fun it is to enjoy nature at its best;
We had chosen Frank Lloyd Wright for this test.

These inspirations had to be recorded on that glorious
morn—
Another gorgeous day in Michigan had been born.

October 20, 1985

NEW ARCHITECTURE

What purpose does the new architecture serve?
What is accomplished by each innovative curve?

First, it is contrary imagination in pursuit of the original,
Striving to create an icon beyond the digital.

The ideas, the new, and the art transmit many future
visions
Into working order and give directions to construction
missions.

New products are born, and novel methods are tried;
And then the free markets will decide.

The laboratories of gifted and talented minds
Will then turn out incredible, unique designs.

Forming many details into a comprehensive plan,
Numerous steps are taken so the buildings can always
stand.

Commercial, industrial buildings, and cities are the
architects' ideal;
Many of their custom houses have an ingenious appeal.

As appreciative clients thank the architects' guild,
The architects plan and then the contractors build.

A CREATIVE ARCHITECT

Very few outside the earthly realm
Have the courage needed to take the helm.

To perceive the inner needs of a valued client
And then form the ideas within one who is self-reliant.

The gift and the development of a vision
Are accomplished by those with this as a mission.

With warmth, smiles, work, and fun,
The creative associates strive for an award yet to be won.

The imagination evolves into a oneness that is drawn;
The schematics unfold, with effort, like a prancing fawn.

These are special people, drafting with pencils themselves.
Look out, world! Another building for the land of the elves!

Architects of this stature advance beyond traditions,
Challenging all by giving new, beautiful renditions.

July 4, 1993

IDEAS OF ARCHITECTURE

Who envisions and creates?
Who gives us those building treats?

Architects are the ones who plan, design, build, and restore—
Taking on assignments and challenges by the score.

Working with builders and pleasing each client,
As professional artists they become self-reliant.

It was a pleasure to attend that illustrious feat
Where architects enjoyed the discussions at the design
    retreat.

Some ninety enthusiastic architects were at their best,
Socializing, learning, and presenting at this fest.

Camp Hayo-Went-Ha on Torch Lake had been waiting
For this meeting of architects and their rating.

These individuals think through and draw with a flair;
Then craftsmen undertake the projects with great care.

The conference agenda showed unique designs on the screen;
Some were pending, some underway, and others a
    completed dream.

Beautiful, practical, needed, original, and carefully
    designed renditions
Were presented and discussed by these architectural
    physicians.

That's how it was at the Michigan Institute of Architects
    retreat—
A yearly gathering where people with talent meet.

September 10, 1994

BUSINESS

TO ECONOMIC TIMES

As the world's economy takes a turn,
We senior members frown with concern.

Living with the competitive human forces,
Trying products and services from various sources.

Working to excel in our own field,
Maintaining motion to build and not to yield.

Climbing over the cycles of change,
Hoping to survive in the long range.

What can we do but observe and invest,
Believing our decisions will be the best?

Thanks, Claude, for sending the current information;
Reality unfolds as a changing equation.

With diverse predictions and findings galore,
Keeping a good attitude is what we implore.

March 4, 1987

THE FEDERAL RESERVE

The numbers change from day to day,
Challenged by the economic forces at play.

The willing minds of all involved
Are humbly mellowed after problems are solved.

The markets become over- and under-produced,
Testing the individuals who may be seduced.

Time and cycles are in their own way,
Beyond most perceptions that can go astray.

Disciplined rules for memory, retention, and action,
If applied and employed, produce a profitable transaction.

Credit is due to the thoughts of all
Who ponder their own work to avoid the fall.

The top honors, then, go to the ones who try,
For they are the ones who know the reason why.

March 22, 1991

THE SENIOR INVESTOR

What does this person financially need?
The words, trust, and actions to justify the deed.

The first information that clients should know
Concerns their investments and how they can grow.

Next, they must have protection for their saving,
Which invariably comes from life's gifts and financial
    behaving.

They need an extra degree of growth in a percentage of
    their worth,
Just to keep up with inflation on this fast-paced earth.

The key factor in investors' avoiding the use of Tums
Is to achieve well-being through good health and incomes.

The careful investor takes his valuable time,
While the asset manager monitors market direction and
    prime.

How important these asset managers have become;
They are now the answer for increasing the savings sum.

July 1995

WHAT IS SUCCESS TODAY?

What really is success today?
Is it just being unconsumed along the way?

It appears to be certain, most will agree—
We enjoy living as a family in a land that is free.

Everyone dreams and builds in their own way
By thinking, planning, and working day by day.

For those who aspire to gain even more,
They have to be the ones going for the big score.

Beyond the right ideas, product, service, and trend teams,
It takes desire, energy, luck, timing, and work, it seems.

Seeking and striving for one's individual goal
Means loving a challenge and paying the toll.

With constant persistence to complete the job to be done,
Watch out, little fellow, the human condition is on the run!

September 1995

AN ODE TO THE NUMBERS CIRCUS

I've been joyfully thinking of each visible number—
The little ones and big ones, which never seem to slumber.

They have become somewhat like a team of acrobats—
Jumping, running, swinging, and advancing to their next
    habitats.

Representing untold tales as they fluctuate,
Who can keep up with those tallies as they begin to
    escalate?

Made of circles, turns, lines, and forming configurations,
Tumbling about and then waiting for their new
    inspirations.

Displayed on cloth, paper, and computer screens,
Showing themselves off like kings and queens.

Those crunched symbols being added, subtracted,
    multiplied, and divided—
Goodness knows why so often they are indignantly chided.

After scanning the figures and studying the bottom line,
No wonder there are all types of facial expressions in
    pantomime.

Let us change this image and watch the action in the circus
    tent
So we can enjoy the happy, prideful numbers during the
    main event.

September 1995

EDUCATION

WHERE TO, EDUCATION?

From their mothers to show-and-tell—
That is human beings as they begin to jell.

First came engraving, stories, paper, writing, and
    knowledge,
Followed by needed schooling, study, and then college.

As parents taught and religion grew,
The faith of being came into view.

Assembling both facts and myths,
Mankind became more understanding as they healed their
    rifts.

Communication developed at a rapid pace,
Benefiting all of the nations and every race.

Examples of the good and bad were shown and told
So that more harmonious lives could unfold.

Coding, telephones, radios, and television
Have all helped to advance the human condition.

Now there are busy computers everywhere,
Performing thousands of tasks and handling any affair.

Education for cleanliness, and order for a better life,
Followed by study, discipline, truth, and less strife.

More complexity, motion, and information to sort out;
It is hoped that righteous ways will win the bout.

Personalities with driven motives for life's roles,
All trying to make their living and reach their goals.

As the next generation takes the plunge,
May the world be rewarded as they lunge.

Grant wisdom to the educators for sound judgment and
    activation,
To be merged with doing for experience and then a
    vacation.

May we as citizens monitor the working systems
    everywhere
For a continuing balance of opportunity and a better life to
    share.

UNDERSTANDING

Through history we have lived with political, religious, and
    ethnic behavior,
Which has driven the wills of many to be braver.

From past experiences we must continue to develop
    understanding
If our world is not to become a place for nuclear branding.

Divisions of thought, belief, hatred, and vindictiveness must
    be overcome
How shall we work to accomplish this in the next
    millennium?

With knowledge, communication, and lessons from the past,
Surely we can apply this wisdom to help make our peace
    last.

Will it take an engineered global force to penetrate the
    problem,
Or should each country be trusted to eliminate its own
    goblin?

Can the United Nations isolate and prevent each dangerous
    trend?
Keeping mankind fair, equitable, and peaceful should never
    end.

Compassion for and understanding the nature of each world
    neighbor
Should rule with fairness and never waver.

Oh! We people who have been given our being and our life,
Why can't we evolve to more harmonious ways than strife?

Let us adopt this peaceful mission as our ultimate goal,
Always working ceaselessly for mankind's happier role.

June 8, 1995

OUR DESTINY

Keep it up from all the countries on the earth,
Serving mankind with our God-given gifts since birth.

Believing with faith in our human mission
And becoming better by praying instead of just wishin'.

As we are tested each day with what we do,
The reality of life sets in with what is true.

Working with righteousness, morals, and ethics to serve,
Then patience for an opportunity to observe.

Moving beyond pleasure and sensuality,
As we commit our souls to loving spirituality.

Listening inwardly for God's thoughts and the wisdom of
    the ages,
We would like to add this poem to life's many pages.

May 10, 1993

THE HUMAN SPIRIT

When events and people go through the day,
It becomes remarkable how we earn our pay.

Each one is born into a life condition
With parents, education, experience, and ambition.

Mankind strives for cleanliness, order, truth, and right.
Are these goals worth the necessary fight?

Teaching and reaching for a perfect being—
Is this the quest most people are seeing?

Levels of energy, desire, want, and need
Motivate us to contribute a good deed.

Degrees of belief and follow-through
Help mankind to excel—is this your view?

As we aspire to lift our souls to a better condition,
May we keep trying to achieve this worthy mission.

February 27, 1993

WISDOM SPEAKS

Oh, everyone now think through the move;
Super plans need this to keep in the groove.

From point to point, analyze the ultimate risk;
Otherwise, chaos will prevail, and it will be brisk.

Fear and act for each financial try,
Applying all rules learned so as not to produce a
    devastating sigh.

Consult and live by your financial experiences and rules.
Remember and use them—they are the tools.

Concentrate and act quickly if the major scenario turns;
You need safety and flexibility if you don't want to get
    burned.

Remember again and again and wait for confirmation;
You can and will do it—the need is restoration.

TODAY AND TOMORROW

Today is here—
Let us all cheer!

We know how we've planned
As we take a stand.

The past and our habits tell us what to do;
Then comes each new day with surprises for you.

Events occur, conversations come, and decisions are made;
We spend time at play and work for which we are paid.

Today becomes now;
Again be grateful, take a bow.

Tomorrow is another day,
With hopes and dreams along the way.

More time on earth, with darkness and light,
Happy to be here, through the Creator's might.

Today and tomorrow, we still have our goals,
Trusting and building to satisfy our souls.

June 1995

FAMILY

OUR MOTHERS

Motion picture actresses are skilled at acting;
And professional women must be exacting.

Many other women work in their respective roles,
Coordinating vast activities to sustain people's souls.

A good mother is tender, loving, and duty endowed,
Sharing her ways, which makes us all proud.

Mothers' endless work and qualities no one can surpass;
Their remarkable contributions are always first class.

Then thanks, dear mothers, for your constant care.
You will always be loved and needed for what you share.

So as we look up to many pretty faces and models,
May we always remember the mothers who fed us warm
    bottles.

GRANDCHILDREN

There are young ones with pep and energy everywhere;
They are grandchildren with all kinds of cuts to their hair.

Running, bouncing, jumping, and with hidden wills,
Surprising us and wondering as they bound over the hills.

They test us with every simple question,
Hoping we will answer correctly at every session.

These boys and girls come to us—"This toy doesn't work!"
And then, "Where are my shoes?" We need a perk!

The little ones need hugs and tender care;
Another look and they are bare.

We are so fortunate to have each loved young one
To enjoy as we watch them develop under the sun.

Twenty cheers for the exciting new generation;
Let us adapt, keep a good attitude, and then take a
    vacation!

August 10, 1994

EVERYONE'S CHILD

There is no greater love and concern than what we have for
    you.
Our primary goal is to help you do whatever you can do.

And yet you have been endowed with unique desires;
With good values comes self-reliance to stoke your own
    fires.

Your dreams and aspirations are up to you;
Separating emotions and logical conclusions should be kept
    in view.

The gifts of life and talents are what each may own;
It is up to us to apply within our harmonious zone.

Every working day we earn and save some pay;
Some we invest and some we stash away.

As people grow into dependence on themselves,
They must use their own ideas when taken off the shelves.

Knowledge, information, experiences, and actions are
    passed along.
After being sorted out, they are the key factors that make
    one strong.

Only you can reason, and only you can run;
Making decisions on your own will be the most fun.

Available wisdom should be your guiding light;
Blending it with experiences of your own, you can reach a
    new height.

Reliance on others' opinions in each business matter
Needs careful thought so that hopes do not shatter.

Therefore, communication and exchange can only help;
If you do not make your own decisions, success may never
be felt.

The above message is what has come to me today;
It may help you become better and build along the way.

May 26, 1992

THE DEAR ONES

There are some deep blue twinkling eyes
With smiles and rosy cheeks—Come on, you guys!

In and out of the white satin sheets,
Jumping on the bed as the mattress squeaks.

Blankets and stuffed animals are carried around,
Some even are missing and are never found.

It is night time, and they should be in their beds;
The parents know it is time—those sleepy heads!

A call, a shout, a cry, and a plea for a story;
Mothers and fathers never receive enough glory.

And then, at last, they go to sleep.
They are dears when finally there is not another peep.

1989

AN ODE TO OURSELVES

After looking through our closets and on the shelves,
We find we have purchased too many things for ourselves.

So we have written down a New Year's resolution:
Not to buy anything else for our own institution.

The commitment has come for consolidation;
Our need is to be careful about how we seek stimulation.

Wait a moment, think of all the fun we have had
While buying all of those things—we should be glad!

And so for the good of body and spirit,
We wish to speak loud and clear so we can hear it;

That we will abide by our contented will—
Credit cards and emotions, be still!

Well, friends, we thought you might like to hear
These promises we have made for our Happy New Year.

54

ODE TO THE REALITY AT "65"

I have arrived at the age of 65—
Oh! So soon, yet happy to be alive.

Just imagine all those years in time—
Day-by-day fun, family, and work—how sublime.

Human beings with energy and constantly in motion,
Being grateful to God for His devotion.

A pause and then an observation from the past,
Remembering the good and the bad, which never last.

The startling scenes we have seen and our travels afar
Include astronauts landing close to a star.

The sounds of horses, automobiles, and jets,
Steaming volcanoes, explosions, and various pets.

Creeping, walking, running, and swimming,
Sailing, racing, training, riding, and trimming.

Enjoying the forests, mountains, oceans, and shore,
The farms, valleys, cities, and much more.

Appreciating the values we were taught to treasure,
We remain humbly thankful for each special pleasure.

These are just a part of our wonderful life—
Enduring untold experiences and a little strife.

The love and understanding we have for all
Far surpass the misgivings when we take a fall.

Some embedded hate, envy, jealousy, and stress,
Trying to rise above all and hope for less.

The ultimate of all love and miracles is born:
A baby, soft and cuddly in its new form.

To see our accomplishments through the "we cans" and "we
    wills"—
Amazing stories in this world and certainly many thrills.

How values and concepts are perceived by each,
And then leaving the old for the new within reach.

Millions, billions, and trillions are the numbers we have
    seen,
While thousands of workers are at their computer screen.

Then times of wonder and a period to stare,
Planning the next action for those who dare.

Envisioning improvement in our world condition,
With appropriate roles for the next generation's position.

Families, teachers, clergy, and employers have set the course
With experiences that come from the daily source.

Peace, clean living, and order for all mankind,
Preserving the earth's environment with a plea to be kind.

Thinking, working, and uniting are the primary goals;
Those who commit will be more productive souls.

I've been prepared by age 65 for many a decision;
My continuing goal is to share my earned wisdom.

May 2, 1988

THE FAMILY CHRISTMAS TREE

The spruce and pine shaped Christmas tree
Is one reminder of another happy season to be.

Grown, purchased, cut, and assembled for the stands,
Those pruned trees are ready for the waiting hands.

The ornaments are placed high and low
So that tinsel and the colored lights can glow.

What a warm and harmonious symbol of family unity
When these decorated trees become beautiful in our
    community.

This is a time for giving, loving, faith, and peace;
Hooray for the human spirit and for this Yuletide release.

FREEDOM

THE PEOPLE ON EARTH

Our rotating earth is like a giant blender,
Mixing and forming all humans until they are tender.

All colors, cultures, creeds, and make-ups,
Backgrounds or wars, thoughts, experiences, and toss-ups.

Each individual going his own way,
Programmed to live for a hopeful stay.

Serving each other for nature's living cause,
The pursuit of happiness, and some applause.

Building a free nation with liberty and reason
While creating a full life for many a season.

There are many enjoyable benefits in this world;
We seek their meanings as they unfold.

With responsibility, order, and understanding,
Let us all keep our great nation outstanding.

Each believing that he is doing right,
With an inner conviction of steadfast might.

With opportunities for education and spiritual devotion,
We are working, striving, and living in faster motion.

Winners and losers both are making history—
Some are right, others are wrong, and some are a mystery.

Nations of peoples mended to their original homelands,
Some with pride and others distant with united hands.

If we all do our part and are the best we can be,
That is all that is asked for you and for me.

October 22, 1988

WHY NOT?

Another thought passed by the other day,
Thinking back about some perceptions and why they stray.

Competition builds each and every nation;
Work, drive, and time complete the equation.

There are many days when cultures and religions are torn
    apart.
As we return to understanding, that is our work of art.

Poor experiences, blame, and prejudices that are handed
    down—
What a shame we are sometimes shackled by these bounds.

Rushed judgments and unconfirmed feelings can hold us
    back;
They sometimes distort our way for lack of facts.

These views and points at times drive the human system;
Inherited characteristics prove we have to keep the rhythm.

And now if we are to take a fair account,
It is truth, order, trust, and love that really count.

Given our work ethic, talent, and ability to fill a role,
We can just do our best to reach each goal.

Some rare events do take place along life's path,
But most wishes are fulfilled with principles that last.

Student of the universe, ask how and then why;
You are a product of what you ask—just remember the
    reply.

What then appears to be the better way
Takes adjusting our wills and doing what we say.

How can one evaluate the performance and worth of the
movers?
Are they prepared to handle the unforgettable doers?

Inward motivations and talents will develop them.
Challenges and setbacks will keep them trim.

The passing and mysterious man—does he believe in
creation?
Is he one who believes in God and our free nation?

Can she take on responsibilities for herself and many
others?
Or do many little events penetrate and get to her druthers?

The stranger in the crowd may be a giving volunteer;
Service above self, an unsung hero—they could be here.

After all, we are grateful for each individual role;
It apparently is Mother Nature's way to unfold.

Questions and questions and wondering who they are;
It makes one happy they don't have to count on a star.

GIFTED

As the human spirit unfolds on earth,
We see the fleeting action as it begins at birth.

What is this inner motion that creates?
Where, when, and how does it originate?

It is a great manifestation that molds the human race,
And it becomes quite wonderful despite the pace.

Evolving into who we are and what we shall become,
Assuredly, it keeps humanity active and on the run.

Some are gifted, lucky, and blessed; others work to earn.
Some are here waiting to be led until they learn.

Again we have to work and think as a global community;
Remember honor, order, trust, and fairness for our unity.

As peace should become our worldly mutual goal,
Survival and better life patterns are best for the earthly
    soul.

So here we are again, with visions of inspiration,
Still believing that we possess the will for the right
    equation.

June 6, 1994

CONSCIENCE

It appears to be the inner personality—
The right of what we all intend to be.

A major voice that questions from within,
Guiding our every action, perhaps away from sin.

This unseen emotional force controls temptation;
With its binding will, it rarely takes a vacation.

Along with the process can come jealousy, envy, revenge,
    and hate;
What a job it is to consistently dispel these traits.

Uncontrolled events sometimes test our worthy way;
Then we overcome, look beyond, and patiently pray.

Rapid signals are sent to keep us righteously straight;
If they are disobeyed, we may be left to fate.

We believe most try to do their best,
But sometimes there are those who defy this test.

With exposure to many thoughts that enter our mind,
It is remarkable how most can come out well timed.

Listen and act carefully, and let your conscience be your
    guide.
You are at the helm; may creation's good gifts be on your
    side.

PEOPLE

PEANUTS AND CHARLES M. SCHULZ

He is a most exceptional human being,
One who captures the moment in what he is seeing.

This gentleman is Charles Schulz; he animates our spirit
With his way of creating a story—we'd like to cheer it.

His drawings and messages are without equal—
Millions of people around the world await each sequel.

All those funny little kids, a beagle, and a bird
Performing their roles, although sometimes they're absurd.

Playing baseball, tennis, golf, and hockey,
They all keep busy with life, though sometimes it is rocky.

Schulz transforms the little folks into a real-life zone,
While Snoopy the wonder dog hides his bone.

Charlie Brown, Snoopy, Shermy, Patti, Schroeder, and Linus,
Lucy, Sally, Frieda, Marcie, Woodstock, and Franklin—all
the finest.

What accomplishments Charles Schulz has attained;
Using his head, pencil, and paper—that is how he has
gained.

Drawing blankets, doghouses, and a baby grand—
One can picture all those things, thanks to his skillful hand.

Perhaps no one has created more daily chuckles
Than Schulz's characters in action—with the use of his
knuckles.

Feathered Woodstock and sunglass-hidden Joe Cool
Bring more smiles and humorous renewal.

Combining kites, pumpkins, and the Flying Ace—
And Snoopy's supper dish—what a treat for the human
    race!

The way he exposes the "Lower" Charlie Brown,
He touches us all many times over with that noun.

With each simple and appropriate real-life situation,
Schulz rates far above most others in the nation.

"Good grief" will long be remembered by Charlie's fans;
It always fits the occasion like high school marching bands.

With Schroeder playing on the baby grand,
Beethoven's Ninth Symphony deserves a full-scale band.

Charles Schulz is a spectacular individual with consistent
    originality.
We appoint him five-star general for enriching every
    personality.

He always makes sure his readers have a good time
By never forgetting holidays with the story line.

With excellent, clear thoughts and dedicated concentration,
Whether it's Spike or the others, his work is a sensation.

Perhaps Charles Schulz can visualize the millions of smiles
    each day,
Which he supplies from Santa Rosa, north of Frisco Bay.

We the people are grateful for his prolific ministrations.
He has charmed our hearts with his skillful creations.

WHO ARE THEY?

The public's in motion, and what do we see?
Many of our kind being the best they can be.

Who are these people, and what do they know?
Will they keep persisting, and be rewarded with a glow?

How they dress and how they appear—
Do they realize what affects their career?

There are those who build and save at a high number,
While others spend and have more fun as they're dumber.

Are these people happy with the way they live their lives?
Will they transcend the comfort zone and risk some dives?

What is their cause or concern of the day?
These humans, are they at work or at play?

How are they oriented, and what must they do?
Could we help them if we only knew?

Do these individuals wait to be told?
Or are they the ones who dare to be bold?

What happenings have they experienced along the way?
And can they clear their minds for the play?

Do these unknowns have abilities to offer to others?
Or does their work depend solely on their brothers?

Just what is inside each wonderful human being?
Where are their values placed, and what are they seeing?

Are they ones who give their thoughts and feelings away?
Or does their calm silence reflect what they don't say?

What exposure to life's patterns have they had?
As they sort out their past, have their decisions been good
    or bad?

AN ODE TO JACK NICKLAUS

The whole world was pulling for Jack that day;
It was at the Augusta National Golf Club matinee—

The tournament where golf shows off the very best;
Twenty-one in the final round began the test.

A game where the swings, shots, chips, and putts all count—
Oh! Those little indented balls, how they sail about!

Immaculate and elegant and one of the finest courses
    anywhere,
The Master's is held in the warm Georgian air.

Our Jack, a true champion from Ohio State,
Was more determined than ever not to abdicate.

His performance that day was without equal;
After rounding "Amen Corner," we knew he would provide a
    sequel.

Pictured fairways were carved through the singing pine,
And thousands of cheering supporters made this drama
    unwind.

Grasping his clubs firmly and with concentration,
Jack overshot the ponds and traps, landing on the greens
    with coordination.

The flags were waving and waiting for Jack—
His son, Jackie, caddying, helped him to be exact.

Uphill on the 18th hole and six under par thirty—
Set the stage as the ball went in—it sure looked purty!

Well, Mr. Jack, the U.S. and British Opens, the PGA, and
the Masters—
What else can we say but to repeat, "You are a super
flabbergaster"?

One can imagine how pleased your kin must be—
Each and every one—proud to be a member of your family
tree.

So to you, Jack William Nicklaus, good fortune and our best
to you—
May you have a happy continuance of the game and many
wins, too.

And when we see your little ball on the wooden tee,
We will know you are ready to play another swinging
symphony.

May 30, 1986

AN ODE TO IRVING BERLIN

What a story, what glory, Mr. Irving Berlin—
How did we know this was all to begin?

A master who composes numerous musical selections,
Enabling Americans to share their loving affections.

Oh, where did this gentleman locate each note
To arrange the beautiful music and lyrics he wrote?

How did he pull stars out of the evening sky
And capture human emotions on the fly?

How did he arrange all those rhythmic meanings
For the enjoyment of all his fellow human beings?

A true artist of genius who has moved feelings and feet
And has given millions of listeners a real Berlin treat.

Enhancing all those with romance and talent,
And bringing out each person's ability to be gallant.

Thanks and highest honors from this poet laureate
For your creation with the ultimate sounds of etiquette.

July 4, 1986

ARNOLD DANIEL PALMER

Our Arnold will always be a favorite son.
He is a great person and golfer, taking his victories on the
  run.

Thousands of steps, swings, hits, rounds, and turns,
Giving us fascinating games up and over the berms.

Those irons, woods, balls, and tees hiding in the bag,
Always wondering how many strokes Arnie will take to
  reach the flag.

And all those spectators lined up along the beautiful
  fairway
In anticipation and applauding the smiling gentleman;
  that is his way.

Let us take Arnold's talent at our time and place
And attach it to the Internet for all to remember and
  embrace.

May all his future hits reach their chosen destination,
Even though some extra swings choose to take a vacation.

September 9, 1994

"MAGIC" JOHNSON

What unseen forces move this young man,
One of the most outstanding athletes in the land?

He is an individual destined to be real;
Something additional is confirmed by his great appeal.

With an exceptional talent and an attitude so rare,
"Magic" likes to score and always shows his care.

Guided by many, he has listened well;
His performance everywhere always seems to tell.

His parents, Jud, Darwin, George, and Charles have been
     his guide;
With their love and understanding on earning's side.

From Lansing to L.A., Magic enjoys the play—
Everett, Michigan State, and the Lakers have made our
     day.

A gentleman who takes time for young people and seldom
     pauses—
Congratulations to him for his dedication to good causes.

Requests from autograph seekers and many well wishers—
This star is one of the greatest basketball swishers.

He is a happy and talented athlete, with a positive smile;
His warmth for his teammates takes on a natural style.

Earvin Johnson, you are a true winner and beyond;
Thanks for your service and your super-fine bond.

Our hopes are high for your continued worthy aspirations;
You're a respected leader and a model for future
    generations.

May 1986

OH, DENNIS!

Warming our hearts and spirits, your thinking makes us
    smile;
Hank Ketcham, we are grateful for your style.

Consistently, your cartoons please our senses,
Depicting many characteristics of that child's defenses.

The cast of Dennis and his friends
Are just enjoying normal childhood trends.

Mr. Wilson's inner feelings are always being tested
By Dennis, the contrarian, with little conscience invested.

And yet that bouncing, fantastic little boy
Provides us with belly laughs and boundless joy.

You, Hank, deserve the golden chime
For stretching your genius with Dennis's overtime.

Your millions of readers are proud of you
For the visions and memories you've helped us accrue.

Many thanks for this much-needed humor;
We all love Dennis, that pesky late-bloomer.

PIANIST VICTOR BORGE

What a guy—he's one of a kind—
That is the Victor Borge mind.

The Steinway grand piano shuddered that night
As the gentleman comedian came into sight.

But the black and white ivory keys were ready,
And the grand piano legs were steady.

On walked the master of improvised talent,
With his stride and a smile so pleasantly gallant.

Soon those outstretched fingers touched the A's, B's, and C's;
Then the tones just ripped and flowed with ease.

In the beautiful selections there seemed to appear
The familiar sounds of a "Happy Birthday" cheer.

A genius with simplicity and in command all the way—
Never before have the laughs and applause remained to
    stay.

What joy, humor, and fun the audience had;
Another top performance at the fine arts pad.

We always laugh when Victor begins to jest.
He's excellent, outstanding—one of our very best!

November 14, 1994

A GREAT, GIVING MAN—ALDEN DOW

We were just reviewing the other day
Alden Dow's philosophy, summed up in his own way.

This gentleman was one great, giving man,
Always thinking of improving life in our free land.

An architect who prepared the diagram for the "WAY OF
    LIFE,"
Illustrating by design and diminishing strife.

Building and going beyond to create an understanding way
By structuring an equation for an awareness to display.

His formula for the evolution of the human condition
Enables one to picture each natural rendition.

Here is the formula for our worldly stay;
Well now, Mr. and Mrs. Public, it is your choice and say.

August 1995

LUCIANO PAVAROTTI

Oh! What a royal gift we have in our Luciano
For all to enjoy, with the orchestra and piano.

The world of Luciano Pavarotti's work stands alone
As his melodious voice creates a deep, rich tone.

Major accolades are due the producers, directors, and cast;
Then come the conductors, applause, and Luciano at last.

Entering, he claps his hands, arms outstretched, a kiss,
        smile, and prayer—
The wonderment of his voice begins to fill the night air.

Distant stars have been known to leave their constellation
To attend a Pavarotti concert at our earth station.

Should we elect him this globe's musical king?
His audience is enthralled as his voice takes wing.

His forceful renditions of the talented composers' songs
Build a loving, stately feeling where each memory belongs.

The musicians who accompany him must have a ball
While giving the instruments their exquisite all.

Pavarotti's presence is stately and commanding
As he gives his romantic selections the magic of
        understanding.

Some say his voice has moved the earth off its axis;
This is one of life's joys for which we don't have to pay
    taxes.

Why, this remarkable artist, while singing *Messa di Gloria*
    by Puccini,
Caused my batteries to pop out and my cousin to drop his
    hot-dog weenie.

January 1, 1996

PLACES

OH, ALASKA! WHAT A GREAT STATE!

Informative, entertaining, and exciting Alaskan travel:
Before your eyes, fantastic experiences unravel.

Unsurpassed and unequaled scenery,
Dark mountain peaks with snow and hills of greenery.

This is the land of the whale, seal, and polar bear,
With many eagles, puffins, and kittiwakes flying through
    the air.

Tempered and humbled by violent weather,
A vibrant state with fire flowers like heather.

The traps, the nets, the hooks—the kill—
The fishermen and hunters in action—sometimes still.

From Juneau cruising the Lynn Channel to Skagway—
This is where many Alaskans work and play.

Northeast of this historic gold-mining town
Are reminders of faded hopes but nary a frown.

In Fairbanks via a stern-wheeler on the Tanana River,
Mary Shields narrates a dog-sled ride that makes one
    shiver.

The musk-ox grazing on the perma frost,
Although a little shabby, they are not lost.

And distant Barrow, near the Arctic Circle,
Where the blanket throw makes one perkle.

The vastness of somewhere and nowhere—
This is the real earth, which presents its dare.

Eating yummy fresh salmon and scanning Mt. McKinley—
To taste and experience them is like having Santa come
    down your chimney.

AN ODE TO IRELAND

Everyone should visit this famous isle
To enjoy a spectacular setting in every mile.

Inscribed hedges of stone and hills so green,
Rolling over the meadows and so very clean.

Whiskey, wool, and many a nature-placed bog
All play a part, enhanced by some picturesque fog.

Castles, abbeys, and rows of houses over the hills—
What fabulous architecture, reflecting such skills.

Genuine and pleasing reflections of polite Irish hearts,
Singing, working, fun loving, and all playing their parts.

Whether in Shannon, Croom, Killarney, or Dublin,
They'll make your spirits rise and keep them bubblin'.

Stout, smiling, and hearty people of Irish soil,
Creating determined and faithful men—forever loyal.

The pleasing names of each colorful city,
Like Skibereen and Derrygonnelly, charm each ditty.

The legends are filled with the harps and guitars,
Reminding us of Irish memories in the stars.

And a hundred stone towers in this Gaelic scene—
Imagine all those little leprechauns building their dream.

So Ireland, with your pride and humble zest,
Bless your shining land—it's one of the best!

May 18, 1989

AN ODE TO MAINE, USA—IN 1992

Historic Maine is on our eastern coastal border,
Invaded by centuries of Atlantic waves, yet still in order.

Vibrant winds initiate the changing seasons,
Instilling heartiness in each for good reasons.

With crafts, antiques, tourists, industry, and fishing,
Helping the people thrive instead of just wishing.

The shore and rolling hills with their colorful trees
Provide the beautiful geography, flowing with ease.

With inlets and outlets that unite the coastline,
Visitors become ecstatic with this time-worn shoreline.

There are puffins, eagles, lobsters, and whales—
Wildlife in motion when using their tails.

Houses with wooden siding and many a shake shingle—
Warming the hearts of those who mingle.

With blueberries and tributaries, it has earned its name;
And appropriately scenic is this great state of Maine.

September 24, 1992

NEW YORK CITY

Have you listened to and watched the walking stride
In this fantastic city of boastful pride?

Sometimes overcast and misty, which sets the tone—
Millions of people, and yet one often feels alone.

Always stimulating and amazing to see,
The millions of inhabitants moving with glee.

We as a nation are reminded of our Constitution;
The Statue of Liberty represents us—what a resolution!

Providing culture and entertainment for her peoples,
And then there are the houses of worship with their tall
     steeples.

Fabulous tall buildings rising toward the sky,
Housing commerce and workers of the world as they try.

Surprising harmonious movements of human beings
     sighted,
Fulfilling their own roles in life and still united.

Financial markets monitored and trending,
Surrounded by deep shadows, with many transactions
     pending.

Taxis, buses, subways, and automobiles are in constant
     motion;
Hidden subways carry thousands of travelers through
     locomotion.

It was a day in spring when I was there,
Observing all New York's wonders with a stare.

Amazing human harmony and awesome architecture in its
    place—
What an exalted experience to be walking in this space!

Spring 1987

THAILAND, 1992

With reverence and respect we discovered Thailand,
A country that is so different from our land.

Fascinating historical kingdoms through the ages,
Many contributing citizens who are imprinted on time's
    pages.

From the cities, resorts, harbors, and farms,
They become vibrant with man's quest for increased
    charms.

Faith, hope, and gracious smiles,
With warm Thai spirits they withstand the trials.

Millions of people work in harmony in their own way,
Accepting life's challenges as they earn their pay.

The Golden Buddha and the Temple of Dawn—
Great masterpieces, each a phenomenon.

Then the spires, temples, palaces, and artful wares,
Creating sensuous overloads, which Thailand shares.

For decades to come, the world will marvel at each artistic
    hand
That has worked to preserve this fantastic, mystical land.

March 27, 1992

BEAUTIFUL VAIL, COLORADO

Accessible to the world, with many a snowy mountainside,
What a place to slalom and ski with pride.

The spruce- and aspen-covered mountain scenes
Are some of the best for skiers' means.

In this Alpine-decorated city of fun,
People in brightly colored ski suits swish down each run.

Creaking snow, compacted and compressed—
These are the sounds for the happy quest.

Perfect snow slopes, combined with the brisk air—
These are the ultimate for those who dare.

The finest selections at the shops and for dining
Have earned for Vail the silver lining.

So when one sees those crystal flakes of snow,
Vail becomes another great place to go.

January 25, 1991

NAPLES, FLORIDA

What a magnificent sunset—
Beyond words, where the earth and sun met!

Many have seen those resplendent colors performing,
Gracefully shifting about and waiting for morning.

It was a pleasant March evening in beautiful Naples,
With flickering candles on the friendly tables.

The palm trees waved at the falling red sun
As our side of the world paused for tomorrow's fun.

Even the Gulf's lazy waves came ashore to rest,
And life itself gave thanks for being blessed.

One could watch the purple sunset span the western sky
As that wonderful day smiled and bid us good-bye.

March 11, 1994

THE SLEEPING BEAR SAND DUNES

The automobiles pull up and park. "Everybody Out!"
The children have arrived, and boy, do they shout!

Ahead is a gigantic Sleeping Bear sand dune,
Waiting for thousands of feet and toes at high noon.

They're all ready for the climb to the top;
Away they go, some never stop.

Having reached the crest on the sands of time,
One can now view Glen Lake reflecting the resplendent
    divine.

The hearts beat faster, and the breathing deepens;
Some run downward, and others come leaping.

Here the air is clear and the sounds ring free;
Toward the west, Lake Michigan is lined with trees.

What a glorious place to visit and have fun—
Another nature-made wonder for a sandy run.

June 14, 1995

UTAH—COLORADO—RAH! RAH!

Leaving Delta, Colorado, past Cathedral Peak,
We headed for Utah's canyon land for a needed retreat.

ARCH'S NATIONAL PARK

There they were, those red, pink, and white arched
    formations—
Beyond our magnificent conceptions and imaginations.

We were immediately overwhelmed and surprised to see
The layers of thousands of centuries worn by Nature's
    dynasty.

CAPITOL REEF NATIONAL PARK

Nowhere else on earth does one see outcroppings like those
    near Capitol Reef—
Another part of never-never land, astounding and beyond
    belief.

Picturing the variations of rocks left from vast eruptions,
Resulting from the forces of inner earth's unusual
    corruptions.

It is always a thrill to see the deer and the proud elk
Grazing in the hills and happy like Lawrence Welk.

BRYCE NATIONAL PARK

It was a beautiful drive to fabulous Bryce National Park,
Where Nature has left her magnificent sculptured mark.

Probably one of the most beautifully colored configurations
   on planet earth,
With pinnacled levels of cathedral spires giving art its
   worth.

ZION NATIONAL PARK

Oh, Zion, you with your massive fortifications—
Majestic, imperial, with your Mars-like formations.

These inspiring works of Nature's ruling might
Transform one's consciousness into an unimaginably rich
   sight.

MESA VERDE NATIONAL PARK

The remains of Indian architecture at Mesa Verde National
   Park
Are another instance where the past has left its mark.

It's amazing to see the dwellings built within the cliffs,
Which the Indians carved out to protect themselves from
   rifts.

Americans, Americans—and friends around the globe:
Utah's and Colorado's national parks are treasured parts of
   Nature's wardrobe.

Everyone should visit these wonderful national parks
To discover and appreciate our earth's mighty monarchs.

SPORTS

At Sarasota . . .
"THE SENIOR'S PGA TOURNAMENT"

Oh PRESTANCIA ! Oh PRESTANCIA ! What a glorious day
on the greens
Carefully trimmed and challenging with a revered
esteem.

Sunny and warm with a slight Florida breeze
The golf course and event were there to please.

It was Senior PGA tournament time and all was ready
The golfing and baseball pros welcomed the games
amoretti.

Guess what happened on the number sixteen green?
It became a site to behold, one we had never seen.

We had the distinct pleasure of watching two holes in one—
That great historical day was so much fun.

Chris Gargano, an amateur and Al Kaline, a baseball star
Raymond Floyd related, "From a home run to a hole in one"
It is better than par.

This time those little white balls spun into the hole
They were destined to be Aces and proud of their role.

What a presentation and performance that perfect day
When the smiling players and spectators had their way.

I AM A GOLF BALL

As I began rolling down the assembly line,
I thought that everything would be just fine.

After being packaged, shipped, and advertised,
I knew quite soon I would be utilized.

When purchased, I was placed in a golf club bag;
It was crowded with tees and had an identity tag.

I really don't know what will happen next;
It is rarely printed in a scholarly text.

Unzipped, removed, and ready to go—
Unaware that I was the main part of the show.

Set up on a tee that was stuck in the ground,
I couldn't help but wonder why I had come around.

Then a sound of rushing air, and I knew I had been hit:
OUCH! OUCH! I thought I'd better pray a bit!

Flying through the air, just missing a bird in flight,
Next I was curious where I would alight.

Bouncing off a rock and then a tree,
It was then I began to question my destiny.

Hearing the clanging of clubs and some conversations,
For me it was not the best of vacations.

A bunker ahead and then a sanding,
Chipped with a swish, a spray, and a soft landing.

After that, I continued on a long, long safari—
In and out of the jungle, as reported in my diary.

Time after time I was analyzed and hit—
Splashed, lost, found—it was just the pit!

Taking a constant pounding time after time—
Oh! For a peaceful destination that would rhyme.

I was putted onto the green and into the hole;
There was a loud shout: "Finally"—what a role!

What a challenging sport golf continues to be!
It's fine for the golfers, but certainly hard on me!

THE GAME OF GOLF FOR TWO

Within me there is a little guy;
He speaks so softly, and I know why.

This inner voice is always with me,
Especially when I'm on the first golf tee.

After study, practice, and advice the game can begin;
It's a time for discipline and a steady grin.

A session of golf needs quiet concentration;
The right program is proven by constant demonstration.

The small white ball waits to be hit;
A swing begins after the rules are confirmed bit by bit.

So the great game of golf continues without end;
All balls land, but we know not where or when.

When spring comes again, our bags, clubs, balls, and tees
    will be ready;
We hope that little guy will be with us and be ever so
    steady.

THE PROFESSIONAL GOLF SOUNDS

The mourning dove began the day,
Cooing as the lady pros came out to play.

With the swish of a club as it hits the ball,
The spectators watch as it begins to fall.

Some individuals shout "Down!" "Stop!" and "Whoa!"
Hoping to control its direction like a generalissimo.

The top players talk to those little round balls;
It is surprising how many obey their calls.

An iron is pulled from the large golf bag;
"Clang, clang" go the others as they begin to sag.

Another skillful swing and a good firm clink—
The divot flies and drops down on the link.

The ball is chipped; it lands softly, spins, and stops;
It's so close to the hole—"Go on!" but it does not.

The flag pole rings as it is lifted from the hole;
The putter is ready and knows its goal.

The pro carefully lines up the important putt;
Thank goodness the green has been freshly cut.

With a concentrated punch, the ball rolls toward the hole.
The crowd yells "No!" "Yes!" "Go in!"—"Ohhh!"

That dimpled white ball has missed again;
No one could have tried harder to go in.

The rest of the time remains calm on the beautiful course;
The challenge, the fun, the companionship are endorsed.

This time that putt is on hole eighteen;
Now the crowd bursts into applause as the winner beams.

The internal practicing and thought control
Are unheard, but are truly commendable to the golfing soul.

June 6, 1993

GAME BALLS

As ordinary people, at times we are abused;
Then we think of the balls used in sports and become
    defused.

Those round objects, which come in all sizes,
Are made of leather, rubber, canvas, plastic, and surprises.

In all kinds of contests they are hit, thrown, and slashed—
Kicked, squeezed, caught, dribbled, pounded, and trashed,

Clubbed, racketed, netted, pitched, and hammered—
Only the players and crowds are enamored.

The materials inside each flying sphere
Are hidden by their covers; when used, they're in high gear.

Consider these objects of play and the treatment they take;
Everyone having fun but the balls—how they ache!

We see them flying through space and sometimes hear
    "Ouch!"
We know why the little kangaroo stays in its mother's
    pouch.

The millions of fans may watch, wave, and yell.
The spectators may be in heaven, but the balls go through
    hell.

November 1995

STORIES

THE NIGHT OF THE CONCERT GRAND

Picture another evening at the beautiful fine arts center,
And then visualize a talented trio as they enter.

To most, they were three gentlemen with unfamiliar names;
In reality, they were musical artists with international
    fame.

The new Steinway concert grand piano was ready;
The professional pianist was confident and steady.

Haydn's, Mendelssohn's, and Tchaikovsky's melodies
Were waiting to be played with seeming ease.

Then all at once the famous trio began—
Oh, how those strings and melodious notes ran.

The ultimate piano had been planned, built, and tried;
The tones released that night were full of pride.

The black and white keys on that concert grand
Danced as they were pounded and played, while carefully
    scanned.

The pianist's fingers were jumping and always in motion.
By gosh, it took so much dedication and timely devotion!

Chamber music was being played at its very best;
The applause confirmed that the Steinway had passed its
    test.

September 28, 1993

111

A TREE—FOLLOW ME

A seed was planted in the soil;
With time and the elements, it grew according to Hoyle.

I was so proud of my many branches;
I had become tall and large, wondering at my chances.

Somehow we all grow to be mature;
This we all know is for sure.

Shh! Who was coming through the wood?
A logger with his chains—there he stood.

Ouch! The chain began to cut, and the sawdust flew.
Down I came with a thud; then my branches were trimmed,
    too.

A heavy steel chain was wrapped around my trunk;
I was pulled over the rough terrain, thumpity-thump.

The crane placed me on the trailer bed;
Off to the lumber mill—enough said.

Oh! Oh! I was dumped on a cold, cold deck.
A short time later, selected and grabbed—what an effect!

Heading toward the mill held by the world's largest fork,
I knew I was in real trouble—maybe a sausage like pork!

"Handle with care" was nowhere to be found.
I was placed on the conveyor with a harsh grinding sound.

Here I am, moving up into the debarker—a revolving
    cutting tool;
Watch out! My bark is being removed, and I could lose my
    cool.

Cleaned and stripped bare and soon to be cut apart;
Firmly set in the headrig—Oh! The noise! What a start!

Have you ever been turned, pushed, and spliced?
That sharp-toothed blade didn't feel so nice.

Carefully selected and cut to get the best grade out of me,
It's tough on my structure, can't you see?

Over the conveyor, slab after slab, and squared off for use—
Little did I realize that my cells could take that much
    abuse.

Side to side, from level to level, what a trip I was on.
The unforgettable noises clunk-pounding—how to respond?

When I was in the forest, two boys were talking about rides
    in Disneyland;
If this was to be one of those, please give me a helping
    hand.

The machinery, steel tables, and framework were quite a
    sight;
I'm glad this movement is during the day and not at night.

All they wanted of me was my best—
Into the shredder went the rest.

I'll never forget how I was treated that day—
Absolutely no respect along the way.

At the final stage, I was stacked and stripped,
Knowing I was destined for another trip.

Gliding on the rails into the kilns to be dried—
Hot and steamy, and what's left of myself again to be tried.

My cells and fibers would never be the same;
The winter and summer growth even changed by this game.

After sweating it out, leaving the kiln and all dried,
I felt so much lighter and ready to be tried.

How would I now be finished—resawn or surfaced on each
    side?
It was up to the orders—where could I hide?

Zipped into the planer and sanded so fine,
I became concerned for my existence—how much time?

And now again sorted and piled onto a bunk,
Joining my separated parts but never again into a trunk.

Stacked, wrapped, banded, and ready to go;
Then loaded into the flat car—on with the show.

The rumbling wheels on the train kept us on track;
Now, I must say, there's no looking back.

After a dirty, wet ride I arrived at the rail-siding.
The two-pronged lift truck was waiting to do the guiding.

And now here I am, inventoried in the yard;
The job site will soon be ready, and me again on guard.

A call comes, and it is clear that I am needed,
Headed for the project where I know I'll be greeted.

The carpenter looks me over to make sure I'm the right one.
Then he carefully carries me to my position—will it be fun?

No! First, I was cut and then I was nailed into;
After all that action, can you believe what I've been
    through?

Pounded and pounded—Oh, look at me!
Now I know how a golf ball feels on the tee!

I am now affixed and finally in place,
Believing I might be seen in this final space.

How proud I was to be where I could be seen
Until a man with a brush painted me green.

What a trip—what a life—what effort—this is my story.
Would you support yours truly for an hour of glory?

May 9, 1986

ONE LITTLE MOUSE

Subjected and directed to creative ideas and travels,
Walt Disney was destined to release historic salvos.

In the beginning there was one little mouse in a big hurry;
Then evolved the vision of playlands for excitement and no
  worry.

Carefully planned for a spacious and fun time of an
  amazing event,
It is where imagination and animation become diligent.

Disneyland and Disney World are accomplished fantastic
  dreams,
Created and built with risk and remarkable artisans on
  many teams.

Successive thoughts assembled an empire of pleasure as
  the Disney domain
For millions to visit and experience with renowned acclaim.

This is where the trams, trains, boats, and monorails
Whisk all the families into cheerful storybook tales.

The thrills, discoveries, and the unexpected
Are there with new sounds, colors, and fascination
  perfected.

The settings, themes, and rides through the tunnels with
  turns
Keep sparkling eyes rolling as the happiness churns.

Bright hues of shirts, caps, mugs, and fuzzy creatures
Await the arrival of enthusiastic tourists and teachers.

Look at the cleanliness, order, politeness, and images, we
ask.
Commendations to all for their part in this momentous
task.

BRAVO! BRAVO! For this human-made paradise of magic
and wonder;
Attendees from around the world applaud it with thunder.

All in all, the Disney parks exalt the harmony of a joyous
spirit,
Forever to be remembered by those who have endeared it.

THE SECOND LITTLE MOUSE

It is not Mickey or the house mouse . . .

It is the little one that directs the cursor all over the screen
Under someone's direction to find the categorical theme.

Controlled by millions of thinking and active minds,
Busily locating the desired subject within the lines.

Point, click, and take aim with the second mouse;
Now it can alter the design of a Frank Lloyd Wright house.

Imagine those little arrows in our technological age,
Providing easy access to the computer instead of the page.

Responding to computer time and now in a major role,
That is the SECOND LITTLE MOUSE, according to our
    poll.

THE THIRD MOUSE

This ode's about a pretty girl named Sue,
Who was sitting in a house of worship—in a pew.

With sparkling dark eyes and a vibrant smile,
She had come to church for just a while.

Sitting behind her was a fellow named Bob.
He noticed a quick swish, and hoped Sue would not sob.

As he carefully touched her, he could see
A tiny little mouse heading for her knee.

A soft yelp—it was just a brief expression—
The readers were surprised; it was not in the lesson.

Joe, Sue's husband, could be found nowhere;
It was hunting season, and he was after a bear.

Imagine that whiskered, long-tailed rodent—
Visiting the sanctuary to become more potent.

This short story would be easier to believe
If that little critter had run up Sue's sleeve.

October 15, 1995

OUR AIR FORCE

If you look into the air over Williams Air Force Base,
You might see these flying turbo jets out in space.

Those two little trainers, the T-38s and T-37s,
Have performed many assignments in the high heavens.

It was a proud day to have our sons arrive
At Lansing's Capital City Airport after a dive.

Each year these jet pilots fly a cross-country test,
Practicing their training procedures to become the best.

Underneath the canopy was the little dual cockpit,
With many controls handy for each flying trip.

Two baby turbo jet engines fly these skilled pilots in precise
    formation,
Strapped into ejection seats—what a sensation!

Controlled by buttons, switches, arrows, and indicators,
These proven trainers are the force's vindicators.

"No Step," "USAF," "Ground Here," "Low-Pressure Oxygen"
Are all imprinted on the sleek riveted aluminum skin.

The captain calmly smiled and looked at this weathered
    plane;
It could have made 10,000 flights and looked about the
    same.

It was a special historic day to see these men come home;
What a beautiful sight on a clear blue day to roam.

Congratulations and honors to these powered G's in flight,
And to the manufacturer and qualified men who keep them
tight.

So someday when you hear that astounding roar,
Look up, smile, and watch to see the Cessna Tweet soar.

REBIRTH OF THE WACO AIRPLANE

November 20, 1985, was a classic day;
Old Man Winter was blowing in to stay.

Notable personages came to see the Waco's first flight,
And they were all pleased with the performance at the site.

An aviator in his black leather suit climbed aboard;
Everything checked out and was in accord.

The engine started, and the plane was swiveled and turned;
That beautiful wooden prop helped as the motor churned.

A small parade followed this brand-new aircraft to its post;
An assortment of doughnuts and cider were there to toast.

Was everything and everybody ready for this test?
Full throttle—100 feet—and up it shot toward the west.

A sweet sound, and the pilot was heard to say,
"Mr. Waco, take me to cloud nine today."

It was off and away in a great flight pattern—
A prized white spectacle somewhat like Saturn.

Brrr! Those heavy-duty rubber bands were cold;
But Classic's new version became a reality after leaving the
    mold.

We are all proud of the team and your accomplishment this
    year;
One could easily tell by the community members' cheer.

As the Waco returned to the point of origination,
There were smiles, handshakes, and then confirmation.

Another great working team has achieved its glory
By custom-building another Waco—that is the story.

THE RED-HEADED WOODPECKER

The red-headed woodpecker is an active bird;
His repetitive tapping is almost absurd.

Rat-a-tat-tat and a rat-a-tat-tat is his knocking sound;
You'd think those old elm trees were headed for the ground!

This colorful woodpecker stands so straight and tall;
With that hardened beak, he has a ball.

So while you're in the woods some sunny day,
You may want to watch a happy pecker pecking away.

April 26, 1995

124

ABOUT THE AUTHOR . . . The man behind these words and thoughts . . . and what *Accolades* will do for you.

Donald Schaberg is just another average fellow who was born on a farm and then moved to the city.

After serving in the United States Navy during World War II, he entered the lumber distribution business. Branching out with ideas to serve the marketplace for a better world for all, as well as traveling, enabled him to work his pen and pencil overtime.

Working with the architect, Frank Lloyd Wright, in designing their house built in the country, Don and his family have lived with Mr. Wright's philosophy: wanting man to live with beauty, to find poetry and romance in daily affairs, and to establish clearly the rights of individual expression.

Don and his wife, Mary Lou, have six married children and almost 21 grandchildren. With many family experiences, business transactions, travel, and reading, the author has had an opportunity to observe many things.

After writing hundreds of poetic acknowledgments, the writer has selected these messages of inspiration about gratitude and wisdom, mingled with innuendoes of fun.

The book is designed to present an anthology of the author's visions, which may enable the reader to sense another dimension in musical words as they sing out their message.

When one has been fortunate, he often asks, "What can I give back to the world besides my work?" With this question in mind, these messages are for you.